Retirement: Start Thinking About Your Retirement

Book 4 of Money: Learning the Basics

Joseph Evaldi

The Books from the Series
Money: Learning the Basics

Going Broke: Learning from Financial Mistakes (Money: Learning the Basics Book 1)

Saving: How to Save Your Money (Money: Learning the Basics Book 2)

Budgeting: How to Budget Your Money (Money: Learning the Basics Book 3)

Retirement: Start Thinking About Your Retirement (Money: Learning the Basics Book 4)

Disclaimer

Otherwise, have fun reading this book. I hope it gives you some ideas that you can use.

Table of Contents

About the Author

Introduction

I am 35 years old and I am approaching 36 years old at this time of this writing. Retirement is 30 years away from me. It's safe to say I have to think about retirement. Like many I didn't plan my future and I lived for the day. I am just lucky enough to have $8,500 saved in my finances.

That is why I am writing this book. I am not screwed yet. I could make decisions that will change my life. And this book can help you to think about retirement like I am now.

In this book I will discuss about the options you have for retirement. I did research on retirement, but I am sad to say I haven't done it fully. However, I am going to discuss what I have learned about retirement.

Many young people like me didn't think about their retirement, they live for today or they planned for the future and they lost their money in 2008 during the crash.

I didn't plan on my future, I just planned here and there and I've been working in two jobs that give me two days a week at the time of this writing. After I left one job, the other job is giving me more hours. This is a reason why I embarked in side hustle with writing.

The fact is when you get older you think more about the future and your older years. There are many options I plan on doing for the future and all we know is that the future is uncertain. That is why no matter where you are in your investment life, 18 years old and starting or 55 years old and ready to retire. There is a chance to develop a plan for the future where you can succeed in your retirement years.

What I won't talk about in this book?

I won't talk about where you should put your money. That is your choice. I will give you suggestions of where it can go that can help you no matter what age you are.

I won't talk about numbers and figures because they can be intimidating even though some numbers are smaller then it seems. Anything can make money, but the idea of compounding will do a lot more and it isn't that much to make much when you think of it.

And I won't discuss about risky investments even though in times such as depression everything is a risk which I will discuss about in Chapter 1.

A Run Down of the Chapters in the Book

In the first chapter, I will discuss about times of financial depression. There are things to do in times of financial stress. Maybe we lost our money from bad investments, or our investment just crashed, or we didn't spend wisely our money. And as time went on we are later at life and we don't know what to do. Some people play the catch up game. This will be discussed.

In Chapter 2, I discuss about not putting all your eggs in one basket. You can't bank on putting all of your money in one place. This will lead you up shits creek and then 1929 or 2008 happened. For people not prepared for the storm, it will hurt in your pockets.

In the Third Chapter, I will discuss about the pros and the cons of the 401(K) or the 403(B). Should we put all our trust in them?

In Chapter 4, I discuss about the different retirement investment options such as IRAs, Insurance, Bonds and Emergency Savings. There needs to be preparation when you retire.

In the Fifth Chapter, I discuss making your money work for you even into retirement. This is the idea of royalties'. Money you can make long after you're gone.

In the Sixth Chapter, I will discuss about setting up your money for your loved ones until after you're gone.

Then in the last chapter, I will wrap up the topics in this book and discuss what to do with retirement. This is a time where you grow old. How do you want to spend it? As I watched in a documentary movie like The Secret, they raised the question, what will your Opus be? In other words, how will you leave your mark on this earth? How will others learn from you?

I raise that question here because after a full life of work and experience in and out of your job, there is something to offer. What will be remembered of you until after you're gone? What mark have you left for others?

This is important and a chapter in itself. Retirement is something to think about and as the promo setting up Wrestlemania 31 between the Undertaker and Bray Wyatt. The Undertakers words were, "I'm not dead yet." He was saying, he might be beaten, but still he has a lot more to offer.

Life is like this. The Baby Boomers are the wealthiest demographic in the Country and even though the young try to move them over, they work and hold onto their spot even more so then the young and ambitious.

The idea of retirement has changed. Who would have thought 20 years later since the internet came on the scene, 11 years after Facebook, and a few years after Twitter; the baby boomers now complain that they don't have a smart phone for them. This is a changing world and thinking about retirement is different. It is a time where you reacquaint with your friends and prepare for your journey home.

I don't mean to make it sound doom and gloom, but you want to make the most of your retirement. Some work until they die and some enjoy life for a span of 20 years. This will be the final chapter in the book.

Retirement is your decision. It is up to you to decide what you want to do with your life. I wish you the best in making your decision.

1

Singing the Blues of the Economic Depression

It was early 2008, everyone said buy a house with little to no credit. Everyone got a house and then the bubble had busted. Flash back in time, it was the year 2000, everyone was making money online and then the bubble busted. Flash back more, 1929 the stock market crashed and the bubble busted. Any point in history in these times, people suffered and they are still suffering today, but in times of suffering great innovations happened.

Right now, we have been prosperously poor. We have a laptop, Cable TV, an iPad or a Kindle, our iphone or smart phone and we can eat and just barely make it with little money. Some aren't moving, but the brilliance in this market is anyone can make money now with the internet. Anybody can spend $20 a paycheck and it will reach out around the world. Picking any location you want. Opportunities weren't there before.

But those who are retiring and have lost their fortune, they have every right to be stressed. They prepared and had it all taken away from them. And they get angrier when they spent the bailout money partying it away with women.

It was interesting times back then. And everyone was in panic mode. They realize the hard way, the retail world wasn't for them anymore and they had to find new opportunities.

I won't lie, in 2008, I was 29 years old and I was heavy in debt. Granted I didn't make the best decisions in my life. But it was the next year that I started to change my perception of how I viewed money and life.

When your back is against the wall it pushes you hard and it pushes you to the limit. You realize your 29 and heavily in debt and you can't move out on your own or can't afford it on your own. Luckily I had my parents, but that was humbling. They always wondered why I hadn't been doing something with my life. This is how baby boomers view my generation. It is tough for us to do it on our own and we need help.

However, the wealth of a generation is tied up and if we don't take care of the elderly it will be taken away from us because the government wants there cut. They don't care about your livelihood and they don't care if you are on the streets as long as everyone gets there money, they are ok.

This is why friends are joining together to survive in today's world. It forces you to make better decisions in life and think about retirement.

For those that are older and lost a portion of their money, they have to work more years of their life.

For example, my Dad is still working with bad hands and bad legs because of expenses that need to be taken care of in the house. Sure he had an insurance plan, but he didn't think about how to supplement his money. For all, he was taught social security was always going to be there. And then it got depleted. People need Social Security, a 401 K, an IRA and an Insurance Plan just to retire. Also, they need emergency money on the side.

It is a lot more expensive to live nowadays. In the area I live in it costs about $80,000 a year to live and I was making $9,000 with help from my parents.

I was also taught you could go far on a college education. I am still paying that debt off and I couldn't find a job that I really wanted to do. I should have never gone to Graduate School. And what I'm doing now is different from what I studied for.

These are the common struggles for everyone. Everyone wants to live in luxury yet we are in debt and as it says in the song Sixteen Tons, "I owe my soul to the company store."

These are the struggles we face and parents are helping their kids to live unless their parents are dead or don't want to help them out.

Or there are rules to abide by. Which raises the question, what is freedom?

I may work two jobs, a third maybe. I might live with a love and if we have children, then I am constantly paying bills to the end. So where is the freedom?

This is where we need to come up with a plan and as Ray Dalio said in Tony Robbins recent book *Money: Master the Game*, there has to be an all season plan. This is why you don't put all your eggs in one basket.

2

Why Putting All Your Eggs in One Basket Isn't a Good Idea for Retirement?

Most people like to think what is easy and what is convenient. I am like most people. It was until my life started crashing down on me that I then realized I have to do something and do something quick. I am like most people who were struck with the fact that they don't have much savings put away for their retirement.

It's safe to say, many people live for today, while some work smarter. That is why it is good to follow David Bach's philosophy by automating everything and it will add up.

This guarantees you will have money put aside and you can allocate it. It is never safe to have all your eggs in one basket. This is how you can go broke because one crash and all your money that you put aside can be wiped out.

This has happened in times of crisis such as in 1929, the 1970's, 1987, 2000 and 2001, and 2008. People banked on the financial systems to be there and they weren't there. They had to do something different. Everyone had to change their ways and start to allocate their money.

In times of depression, it challenges you to think

outside the box. It forces you to strategize what you can do with your life. In times like this you reevaluate what's going on with your situation and find a better solution to life's problem. Some resort to peaceful protest and some may resort to rioting. I know the Baltimore problem now stems from a greater picture of what is going on in America.

In times of unrest there is stress all around the country. It is a great time to make some changes. This is where great innovations happen. It challenges you to make plans to reinvest. This can be through going to college and re-educating yourself. This can be through investing your money on a talent you have that you might want to excel in.

And if you're in your 50's and 60's maybe you want to take up something different then what you've been doing. Maybe it is something you've always wanted to do, but never got the chance to do.

Also, with allocation, you can decide how to put aside your money. There is the 401(K) and there are IRA's, Insurance, bonds, and other investments you could make to, but I will focus on the 401 (K), the IRA's, Insurance, and Bonds.

In the next chapter, I will discuss the previous history of Social Security, Pensions, and the Pro's and Con's of the 401 (K) and 403(B).

3

Social Security, Pensions, and the 401(K)

In this chapter, I will discuss the back story of the Social Security, the Pensions, and the 401(K)

Social Security

When FDR became President of the United States of America in 1932, he came up with The New Deal. It was a way to put Americans to work again and change the way we think about retirement. It was then Social Security was born.

Social Security at the time was the end all solution to an ongoing problem. Back then things were affordable, housing was affordable, and even if you were poor you could afford to eat.

Times were different then. If people were lucky, then they lived past 70 and they would retire at 65 years of age. Then things changed as the years went on. People's health got better and they were living well into their mid 80's. Social Security had to last 20 years for people. How could Social Security last? This is where companies stepped in to help assist Social Security. So things would be better when people retired. There had to be another supplement other then Social Security. That's when companies issues Pensions as a part of their policies.

Pensions

A friend had told me, who has just retired a year ago; he wasn't sure when pensions came about. He said, "It might have been in the 1950's or early 1960's." He also said that companies had to do something for their employee's retirement when they got there.

Pensions were there to guarantee that the employee's were secured with their retirement. Pensions helped their families even after they were gone. It was a way that companies gave back. They realized things were changing and they cared about their employees. Things had to be different than before. It was around this time that credit cards were born.

However, in the 50's and 60's, they were the WWII generation didn't believe in credit, they survived through The Great Depression, but their kids, the Baby Boomers who were just getting started it was another story. They were about to max out all their credit cards. They were going to live life to the fullest and they started thinking about retirement later in life.

You may ask why I am talking about credit cards and pensions with Baby Boomers. The fact is that things have gotten expensive for the Baby Boomers and they needed those pensions to pay for their debt they accumulated over the years and not just the debt of theirs, but their children, who also lived it up and went to college. That generation has loans they can't pay for.

The fact is money has not been taught and it is abused. I was one who abused money as well and I now pay that price, but it is not too late for me. It is not too late for anyone.

However, the fact is in the 80's they realized they needed something else. They needed to teach this generation that they needed to save money and they needed to prepare for their future and then the 401(K) was born.

401(K)'s and 403(B)'s, Saving for Retirement

In the 1980's, debt was growing and life spans were extending. Social Security wasn't as guaranteed, there had to be something else. Companies had to reward their workers for everything they saved so they matched their efforts.

However, in the 1990's and 2000's, pensions were starting to get phased out. People were comfortable for awhile, but they would be penalized if they withdrew money for their retirement.

They would have to pay taxes on it and then, when they were safe and secure, it was all about to crash down on everyone including the Baby Boomers and it forced them to go to work again or work longer into the retirement years. The 401 (K)'s crashed as the Stock Market went down.

This was in 2008, The World was about to change. This forced people to think differently about retirement. The job sector changed to. The hours weren't there as much as before. This was true with retail. They were pushing everything to part-time and it forced retail workers to find a better way. Our benefits were taken away from us. We even lost our money.

Many of us now have money in retirements that is almost depleted because of down turns in life. And this era is a tough time to live depending on where you live. You are forced to do something different to live nowadays. You are challenged in life.

And that is why you should start thinking about where to put your money no matter how old you are.

In the next chapter, I will discuss about IRA's, Insurance, and Bonds. Alternative means of retirement funding.

4

IRA's, Insurance, and Bonds, Alternative Ways of Saving for Retirement

As I mentioned in the previous chapters, there are problems for people who are unprepared for retirement. They are not prepared for the tides that come in. They need an alternative way or an alternative means to prepare for retirement. Unfortunately, many people don't know that they have options or where to go for their options.

Some would think lets go to the bank, but the bank might not give them the best options. That is why research is needed and there are places to go for that, but the best thing to do is ask around and find the best options. This is what I am trying to do right now once I get enough money together.

Everyone thinks you need a lot of money to make a lot, but it's actually the other way around. You just need a little bit to make a lot. I will use coins for example. I started the year with $0 in change and just by not spending it and counting it and wrapping it, I accumulated $100 in change wrapped. Imagine just putting at least $25 or $50 aside every paycheck and it compounds, that will add up.

This is why I will first discuss about the Traditional and

the Roth IRA first.

Traditional and Roth IRA's

Individual Retirement Accounts or better known as IRA's is your way to take control of retirement in your own hands. You can make contributions whenever you want or have it automatically deducted in the time periods you suggest. You just have to know what each IRA will do.

In a Traditional IRA according to Bank of America's Website:

- Contributions and earnings may be withdrawn without a 10% additional tax at or after age 59 ½

- Contributions may be tax-deductible

- Withdrawals must be taken the year in which you turn age 70 ½

In a Roth IRA according to Bank of America's Website:

- Contributions (not earnings) can be withdrawn tax-free at any time

- Contributions are not tax-deductible

- Qualified withdrawals are federally tax-free and may be state tax-free after age 59 ½ and account has been open five years or more

-     No income restrictions required on converting a Traditional IRA to a Roth IRA

Information about Traditional IRA and Roth IRA was quoted word by word from the Bank of America website. More information on this topic can be found at https://www.merrilledge.com/retirement/ira?src_cd=bac_hp_nav_ira.

The choice is up to you, this is your retirement. But this is a good way to supplement your retirement and have you not working harder into your old days. David Bach discovered if you could only automate it. You will not be working until you are dead and that is the worst feeling.

2008 changed the way we think about money and it is forcing us to think about retirement. That is why I am rolling over my struggling 401(K) from JCPenney after I leave and putting it in Valic, a retirement company, that I've worked with for years. There might be better options, but I am sticking with them.

I like the fact that they invest money in with Vanguard which is a low interest fund company. It has done well as Tony Robbins mentioned in his book and I want my money to work for me as I start investing for retirement.

IRA's are a good way to put money aside while you are

putting money aside in your 401 (K)'s. You want your money to work for you and in an IRA you can do this.

Another means of Retirement is putting your money in an Insurance Policy.

Insurance Policies

I know little bit about Insurance Policies, but I know that things have changed with it. Insurance Policies are a way to supplement your end years and after your gone.

Insurance plans out what happens after you are gone, your funeral and also leaves your loved one with money that could possibly last until after they are gone. To compare it to wrestling, it is like the Money in the Bank contract and once cashed in it will provide.

Insurances also help you in times of hardship and possibly disability. They can help out. As Tony Robbins mentioned in his latest book on money, there are Insurance Policies that will give you money and keep on paying you while you are alive as long as you have invested in it. Like I said, the Insurance Policies are like the Money in the Bank Contract and it can be cashed in when you need it.

I don't mean to talk about wrestling terms, but it is true. You just have to research which one work the best for you.

Next in retirement there are Bonds.

Bonds, Short-Term and Long-Term, Storing your Money for a Later Date

Bonds are a way to store your money for a future date. You only earn small amounts of interest, but they are better than certificates of deposits.

There are bonds which can be invested up to seven years and a Long Term bond which is up to 30 years. This can be another way to supplement your retirement. Interest may or may not be there, but it can help.

You could get company bonds or bonds from a Bank. Again, you need to do research on what's best for you. Bonds might work for you and if money is not there and you have a bond. It might just pay off.

There are other ways to supplement your retirement such as annuities and stocks, but it's up to you decide what will benefit your situation and what will work for you.

In the next chapter, I will discuss another method of help for retirement and that is money that will come in for you until after you are gone and that is royalties.

5

Royalties: The Gift that Keeps on Giving until After You are Gone

You may ask, why did I add royalties with this discussion on retirement? I added most of the essentials, but why royalties?

In my honest opinion, royalties are gifts that keep on giving until after you're gone. You could make music, movies, and documentaries, become a writer and write books. The sky is the limit. And for every purchase of your stuff, there is a small royalty that will be paid.

Even if you are not a famous author and you earn a royalty of about $50 each month, those royalties can help with expenses along the way, especially if you aren't making income anymore.

Royalties are also your hard work paying off. Maybe it will be little or maybe it will be a lot, but royalties will help out. So if you have a project you are working on, it might pay off in the future and it might secure a little income after you are retired.

6

What Will You Do With Your Retired Life?

This is the age old question. You're 60 or 65 years old and you have enough to retire, do you continue working? Do you focus your attention of a hobby you love? Do you spend time with your grandchildren if you have any? What do you do?

This is just the tip of the iceberg with questions to ask for those that are retiring. Right now the Baby Boomers are approaching this age. They have done so much for the world in innovation and development that they have to pass the torch and that is not an easy task for those who were on the top and will die on the top.

My Dad is one of the earliest Baby Boomers and he is still working and my Mom is retired. They both approach retirement in different ways.

Now that it is expensive and bills have to get paid, they do what they can do in their retirement years.

What can you do for your retirement? I know what I am going to do; it is working on my writing, but not working any job.

This is the benefits of retirement, you can work on the side passions you've wanted to do when you are done working. You also have the time to watch your grand children's games. This is the advantage of retirement.

However, what does one want to do with retirement? What is the legacy you want to leave behind? What will you be remembered for? Will it be that job that you do? Or will it be for something that you left behind to someone? There are many things that can be done.

Will you leave this world a better place than when you came here? This is the question that everyone asks in their retirement age.

In retirement you have time to leave your Opus to the world and help your fellow man. You can donate money for a special cause that is dear to you and your family. You might want to help someone with an illness that they have.

The truth is retirement is a time where you can be bitter about your life and live regretting on past mistakes or it can be a time where you can prepare for the next life you go to after your gone.

People have contemplated this since the beginning of time, but it all matters what is left behind and who is helped based on your money if any is left behind.

Some people don't have that luxury to enjoy their retirement. Some are still working doing jobs that don't want to do. This is because they either didn't plan or lost their savings with the crash.

Someone was telling me who was retirement specialist that we were in a depression even though no one was calling it that. And it was longer than the Great Depression period.

People who are retiring now have these questions piling up. They have to face a new reality and that's dealing with the world they created.

What did they create?

Conclusion

I am a child of the Baby Boom Generation. They wanted the best for their children. They developed more for the World that they changed the face of the world.

Now on a side note to answer the question what did they create? Computer advancement wouldn't be possible if it wasn't for them. They defined the way we look at the medical field. I was a counselor in a Group Home setting and 10 years ago everything was hand written. They weren't sure if they could trust the internet or case notes being on the computer.

Times have changed, this world has changed. Numbers are just punched into a computer and that is our paycheck. Thanks to Steve Jobs, Bill Gates and other Baby Boomers who have come, the way we perceived the world has changed. Those that remember what is was like before the internet like me, still remember how it was back then.

I remember when I went outside and played without having fear something might happen to me. I also remember playing the earliest video games and I am 35 years old at the time I wrote this. I remember a feeling called being bored something we don't experience much of today. When I grew up those feelings were good.

This world and its innovation solved a problem, but created another one. Baby Boomers were going hard and they never planned on retiring that is why some still work to this day.

They have done so much for this world that it leaves the biggest population in history reaching retirement age. This is the generation that now complains that they want a smart phone or an Iphone big enough for them all kidding aside.

This is a changed world we live in. We don't experience the peace we had as kids. We work and then work some more. Even if we aren't working, we are working. We are on Facebook, YouTube, or any other social media engine taking our time. We are already in the future. We don't have to look at Back to the Future 2 because it is here. We have picture and picture TV, we can talk to someone on the phone and have someone see us on the other end with Skype or the IPhone.

It is amazing how far we have come in society. Yet the problem is how can you top that? This was a society that spawned the greats of Wayne Gretzky and Michael Jordan. Also, spawned the legends of wrestling such as the great Vince McMahon, who revolutionized how we look at sports entertainment and he is not slowing down. It also spawned the greats in wrestling such as Ric Flair and Hulk Hogan, two icons and that generation that followed. Also, all sports in that period of the 1980's and 1990's.

Now, you don't know who some of these athletes are

anymore.

Which leaves the question of impact on this world for Generation X's, they never made their impact on the world. All of it was shadowed by the Baby Boomers. And the generation after them had partied their way through life. Many of them are in the system as we speak.

Why am I talking about all of this? Well, this is a new way and a new world. It is a world where our every move is monitored thanks to the Patriot Act. I guess it was headed in that direction and now there is unrest. There are people protesting wrongful treatment on every end. People are taking a stand and want to change things. It is reminiscent of the 60's all over again. Some have their ways of fighting.

In 2008, when everything was happening I was on the verge of anger of what went on and maybe I still am, but I sought out a different way that changed my life. I resorted to writing. And this is where the direction of my life has gone.

I've fought against consistently bashing the world we live in. It is a great place and it is never too early to think about retirement even though now times are uncertain that is why I bring this up.

However, I have to say we always live in uncertain times, but if we learn from those before us and we don't panic when in a crisis situation, then things can go better for us as a whole.

We need to plan and strategize like I heard somewhere before, it takes a little bit to make a lot. Every little bit to contribute spreading it out. And the power of compounding it will grow over time.

Many don't think like this. Many nowadays don't want to worry about their future. Many don't even want to know what they have saved up for retirement. This is a problem. I wasn't smart enough to think about my future, but it pushed me in the direction that I am in today.

My biggest reason why I am writing this book is to break through to people of all generations and say it's never too late. If you are older, then you can start over again. If you're my age, then you still have time left, start over again. If you are 18 years old, learn from our mistakes and start putting aside for retirement, you won't regret it.

Don't worry what you will need with your money and if you out live your money. Just make sure your loved ones are secured. Isn't this the key to life? By making sure your loved ones are secured when you pass. Many don't have that opportunity. Some have everything taking away from them. I guess you don't want that. That is why I entitled this book *Start Thinking about Retirement.*

Preview

Going Broke: Learning from Financial Mistakes (Money: Learning the Basics Book 1)

Introduction

You are probably wondering why I am naming the title of this book Going Broke. Well, this book is about going broke and I will show you techniques of how to go broke. You may ask, why do I want to know how to go broke, I already am broke, I want to learn how to make money.

The truth is we all want to know how to make money, but most of us in America are plagued with being broke. We have jobs that pay us too little, or we have jobs that pay us too much and we are drowning in debt. We have not learned what to do with money. And we struggle. Only the wealthiest in the world have figured out what to do with money.

I first want to discuss what this book is not. It won't give you statistics and data of how much people are poor and are in debt. But it will discuss why people are in debt and why I'm in debt.

The fact is as soon as you are 18 years old and you work they swarm you with credit cards. They know you don't know what you are doing financially and they know you will act on impulse. This is some of what this book will discuss about.

The other part will discuss about some other financial mistakes we make. This book will be the first of five books in the series. Other books will be about saving, budgeting, investing & retirement, and residual income.

Why are these books important and what gives me the authority to write about these books. First I want to repeat that I am not an expert and I have failed with money. However, there have been others who have been in worse shape than me. The reason why I am writing these books is to implant these ideas in my head and my hope that I will escape my situation and live a better life than I am right now and have my money work for me. I guess this is all of our goals and why America is still holding onto a dream that doesn't exist at the moment.

Everyone in this country got greedy. I am included. In this first book it will be about our mistakes and going broke. First part of the book will be about credit card debt. Second part of the book will be about addictions, such as coffee, caffeine, sex, alcohol, drugs, and gambling and even fast food. All money traps are created through these addictions. The third part of this book will be about the mistakes of Keeping up with the Jones's and why we are in this financial mess. Fourth, I will discuss about poor investments. Finally, I will summarize these topics and discuss about living on impulse and what damage it does.

These topics in this chapter alone could cause someone to go broke. And before we learn how to get out of our situation, we need to be taught about the troubles we all face.

What I Hope to Teach you In this Book?

What I hope to teach you is how we go broke to learn from our mistakes. I believe in karma and a financial system is a form of karma. Whatever we do comes back to us. If we credit that purchase, then we have to pay it back. It is the same thing with a good deed. Sometimes we get swindled. We feel we are helping, but we actually hurt in the end. These are just lessons we have to learn just as I have to learn.

This is why the other person is living such a good life now and you are poor. And other means of impulse as well. You need to not fall for the trap in money and learn to say NO to someone, to that purchase, to that addiction. If you can do that then you are doing for yourself. I learned some of this at 35 years old and still I feel like I am starting over again.

Bottom line, I want to ask the question is that price worth it. Do you want to pay so much and be in debt or do you want to pay the price and owe your lives to a dream that isn't your own. This is something I want you to think about.

If you are in debt, you can reinforce yourself of these mistakes and try to start making plans about how to get out of your situation. This book in the series will start you on that path. So good luck on your journey and learn about our story the American story of Going Broke.

Books Written By Joseph Evaldi

Fiction

A Soul Warrior's Journey

The Day at the Bismarck Herald: The Newspaper Reporter

War

Christmas Fiction

Finding Christmas: The Story of Joseph

Non-Fiction

Birth Order: How the Roles of Each Sibling are Placed at Birth?

The World of Groups: Sociology and My Experiences in Senior Seminar

The Amazing Effects of Water

The Enlightened Way: How the Zen Path Can Help Treat Depression?

Applying Your Own Interests to Your Boring Job: Can It Be Done?

Poetry

Apparitions of a Warrior

Websites for Joseph Evaldi

http://www.facebook.com/Josephevaldi

https://www.youtube.com/channel/UCSp2TBz566yOGiQfLf
k0Zog

http://www.twitter.com/passageofjoe

http://www.amazon.com/Joseph-
Evaldi/e/B00ONSPVQI/ref=sr_ntt_srch_lnk_1?qid=14179608
24&sr=8-1

About the Author

Joseph Evaldi graduated from Kean University studying Sociology. He ventured in with writing with his book The Amazing Effects of Water in 2009.

He then wrote his first novel A Soul Warrior's Journey in April 2013. He later finished writing a book of poetry called Apparitions of a Warrior in July 2013.

In December 2014, The Amazon Kindle book Birth Order: How the Roles of Each Sibling are Placed at Birth? Was the hot new release under Sociology of Marriage & Family for Amazon.

He is currently working on a string of short ebooks which will be released on Amazon Kindle this year.

References

Bank of America.
https://www.merrilledge.com/retirement/ira?src_cd=bac_hp_nav_ira. 2015

Bach, David. *The Automatic Millionaire*. 2004. Broadway Books: New York.

Robbins, Tony. *Money Master the Game 7 Simple Steps to Financial Freedom*. 2014. Simon & Schuster: New York.

www.ingramcontent.com/pod-product-compliance
Lightning Source LLC
Chambersburg PA
CBHW071016180526
45168CB00003B/1445